AURORA SKY

The Neuroscience of Manifestation

*The Magic of Mind and the Science of Achieving Your
Goals*

Contents

X   Practical Applications and Techniques

I

Introduction

1

Purpose of the Book

Ever wondered how our thoughts shape our reality? Or how that whole 'law of attraction' thing really works? Well, that's what we're about to unpack in this book. But we're not just going to throw around some fluffy, wishy-washy ideas. Nope, we're diving deep into the science behind it all – the nitty-gritty of how our brains tick and how that influences what we manifest in our lives.

Now, before we get too deep into it, let's set some things straight. You've probably come across some pretty wild claims about manifestation out there. You know, stuff like "manifest a million bucks overnight" or "attract your soulmate in 24 hours." And while those stories might make for good clickbait, they're not exactly rooted in reality.

That's where we come in. We're here to separate the fact from the fiction, the science from the woo-woo. We're going to explore what neuroscience has to say about manifestation – what's backed by solid research and what's just a bunch of hype.

But why bother, you ask? Well, that's a great question! Understanding the neuroscience behind manifestation isn't just about satisfying our curiosity (although that's definitely part of it). It's about empowering ourselves to take control of our lives, to create the reality we want, and to live our best lives possible.

So, buckle up, because we're about to embark on a fascinating journey into the inner workings of the mind, where science meets manifestation, and where the possibilities are endless.

2

Overview of Manifestation

Alright, let's kick things off by getting on the same page about what manifestation is all about.

Manifestation and its common interpretations

Manifestation, simply put, is the process of bringing something into existence through our thoughts, beliefs, and actions. It's about turning our dreams and desires into tangible reality. Now, you've probably heard a lot of different interpretations of what manifestation is – some folks think it's all about positive thinking and wishful thinking, while others see it as tapping into some cosmic energy to bend the universe to our will.

But here's the thing – manifestation isn't just about sitting around and daydreaming about what we want. It's about aligning our thoughts, beliefs, and actions with our goals and desires so that we can actively work towards bringing them into reality.

A brief history of manifestation practices across different cultures and philosophies

Manifestation isn't some new-age fad – it's been around for centuries, popping up in different forms across cultures and philosophies around the world. From ancient spiritual traditions to modern self-help movements, the idea that our thoughts can influence our reality has been a common thread throughout history.

Take ancient Eastern philosophies like Buddhism and Hinduism, for example. These traditions have long explored the concept of 'mind over matter,' teaching that our thoughts have the power to shape our experiences and create our reality.

Similarly, in the West, thinkers like Ralph Waldo Emerson and Napoleon Hill have explored the power of positive thinking and visualization as tools for achieving success and happiness.

So, how exactly do our thoughts influence our reality? Well, that's where things get really interesting! See, our brains are incredibly powerful machines, capable of processing vast amounts of information and creating complex neural networks. And it turns out that the thoughts we think – the beliefs we hold, the attitudes we adopt – actually shape the structure and function of our brains.

But it's not just our brains that are affected by our thoughts – our actions and experiences are influenced too. When we consistently think and act in a certain way, we start to create patterns in our lives that reflect those thoughts and actions. It's like the old saying goes – "Whether you think you can or you think you can't, you're right."

So, by understanding how our thoughts influence our reality, we can start to harness that power to create the life we want. And that's exactly what we're going to explore in this book – how the science of neuroscience can help us unlock the secrets of manifestation and unleash our full potential.

Ready to dive deeper? Let's keep going!

3

Introduction to Neuroscience

Alright, let's lay down some groundwork and get familiar with the incredible organ that is our brain.

A basic introduction to neuroscience

So, what exactly is neuroscience? Well, it's the scientific study of the nervous system – that intricate network of cells and fibers that make up our brains and bodies. Neuroscience explores everything from how neurons communicate with each other to how our brains control our thoughts, feelings, and behaviors.

Our brains are made up of billions of nerve cells called neurons, which are constantly firing off electrical signals and communicating with each other through chemical messengers called neurotransmitters. These neurons form complex networks, allowing us to think, feel, and experience the world around us.

But here's where things get really fascinating – our brains are incredibly adaptable. They have this amazing ability to change and reorganize themselves in response to new experiences and information. This phenomenon, known as neuroplasticity, is what allows us to learn new skills, form new habits, and even recover from injuries.

Why understanding the brain is crucial for exploring manifestation?

Alright, so now that we've got a basic understanding of how the brain works, you might be wondering – what does any of this have to do with manifestation?

Well, here's the thing – manifestation is all about the mind-body connection. It's about understanding how our thoughts and beliefs influence not just our mental state, but our physical reality as well. And guess what? The brain is ground zero for all of that action.

See, when we talk about manifesting our desires, what we're really talking about is rewiring our brains. We're talking about creating new neural pathways that support the thoughts, beliefs, and behaviors that align with our goals. And to do that, we need to understand how the brain processes information, forms habits, and creates our lived experiences.

By delving into the field of neuroscience, we can start to unravel the mysteries of manifestation – how our thoughts shape our reality, how our beliefs influence our actions, and how we can use that knowledge to manifest the life of our dreams.

So, if you're ready to unlock the secrets of your mind and

unleash your full manifesting potential, you're in the right place. Let's dive in and explore the fascinating world where neuroscience meets manifestation!

II

The Brain and Thought Formation

4

Neural Pathways and Synapses

To understand how our thoughts can shape our reality, we need to start with the basics of how the brain functions. This all begins with neurons and synapses.

Neurons, synapses, and how they communicate

Neurons are the fundamental building blocks of our brains and nervous systems. These specialized cells are responsible for receiving, processing, and transmitting information throughout the body. Think of them as the brain's messengers, constantly delivering signals and instructions that control everything we do.

Each neuron is composed of three main parts: the cell body (soma), dendrites, and an axon. The cell body contains the nucleus, which houses the cell's genetic material. Dendrites are branch-like structures that receive signals from other neurons and pass them on to the cell body. The axon is a long, slender projection that carries electrical impulses away from the cell body to other neurons, muscles, or glands.

The real magic happens at the synapses, which are the tiny gaps between neurons. When an electrical impulse (action potential) travels down the axon to the synapse, it triggers the release of neurotransmitters. These chemical messengers cross the synaptic gap and bind to receptor sites on the dendrites of the receiving neuron, allowing the signal to continue its journey.

Synaptic transmission and the formation of neural pathways

Synaptic transmission is the process by which neurons communicate with each other. It starts when an action potential reaches the end of an axon, causing tiny sacs called vesicles to release neurotransmitters into the synapse. These neurotransmitters then bind to receptors on the receiving neuron, creating a new electrical impulse that travels down its axon. This process repeats, creating a complex network of communication that underlies all our thoughts, feelings, and actions.

As we go about our daily lives, our brains are constantly forming and reinforcing neural pathways – networks of interconnected neurons that represent our habits, memories, and learned skills. When we repeatedly think or do something, the connections between the involved neurons become stronger, making it easier for the brain to activate that particular pathway. This is why practice makes perfect – the more we repeat an action or thought, the more ingrained it becomes in our neural circuitry.

Neural plasticity and how experiences shape the brain

Neural plasticity, also known as neuroplasticity, is the brain's remarkable ability to change and adapt in response to new experiences, learning, and environmental influences. This ability is what allows us to learn new skills, recover from brain injuries, and adapt to new situations.

There are two main types of neuroplasticity: structural and functional. Structural plasticity refers to the brain's ability to physically change its structure, such as forming new synapses or strengthening existing ones. Functional plasticity, on the other hand, involves changes in the brain's functional properties, like how different brain regions activate and communicate with each other.

Our experiences play a crucial role in shaping our brains. For instance, when we learn a new skill, such as playing a musical instrument or speaking a new language, our brains create new neural pathways to support that activity. Similarly, when we repeatedly practice positive thinking or visualization, we reinforce the neural networks associated with those thoughts and behaviors.

This is where the power of manifestation comes into play. By consciously directing our thoughts and focusing on positive outcomes, we can harness the brain's plasticity to create and strengthen neural pathways that support our goals and desires. In other words, we can rewire our brains to become more aligned with the life we want to manifest.

Understanding these fundamental concepts of neuroscience is essential for unlocking the potential of our minds and effectively practicing manifestation. So, let's dive deeper into the fascinating world of brain regions and how they contribute to our thoughts and actions in the next section.

5

Brain Regions Involved in Thinking

Now that we've covered the basics of how neurons and synapses work, let's explore the key regions of the brain that play crucial roles in our thinking, memory, and emotions. Understanding these regions will help us see how our thoughts can influence our reality through the process of manifestation.

Overview of Key Brain Regions

The brain is a highly complex organ composed of many different regions, each with its own specialized functions. Here are some of the most important regions involved in thinking, memory, and emotion:

Prefrontal Cortex (PFC): Located at the front part of the frontal lobe. The PFC is involved in complex cognitive behaviors, decision-making, planning, and moderating social behavior. It plays a key role in executive functions such as problem-solving, controlling impulses, and setting goals. This region is essential for focusing attention and managing thoughts, making it critical for the process of manifestation.

Hippocampus: Located deep within the temporal lobe. The hippocampus is primarily associated with the formation and retrieval of memories. It helps us encode new information and recall past experiences. This region also plays a role in spatial navigation and understanding the context of our experiences. When it comes to manifestation, the hippocampus is important for visualizing past successes and imagining future goals.

Amygdala: Location: Located near the hippocampus in the temporal lobe. The amygdala is crucial for processing emotions, especially those related to survival, such as fear and pleasure. It helps us recognize and respond to emotional stimuli. The amygdala also plays a role in forming emotional memories. Emotions are a powerful component of manifestation, as they can amplify the impact of our thoughts and intentions.

Anterior Cingulate Cortex (ACC): Situated between the limbic system and the prefrontal cortex. The ACC is involved in emotion regulation, decision-making, and impulse control. It helps us manage emotional responses and stay focused on long-term goals. This area is particularly important for maintaining motivation and perseverance in manifestation practices.

Basal Ganglia: Located deep within the brain, near the thalamus. The basal ganglia are involved in habit formation, motor control, and reward processing. They play a key role in developing and reinforcing routines and behaviors. For manifestation, this region helps in creating and maintaining positive habits that align with our goals.

By understanding these brain regions and their functions, we can see how our thoughts, emotions, and behaviors are interconnected. This knowledge is crucial for effectively using manifestation techniques, as it allows us to harness the power of our brains to create the reality we desire. In the next section, we'll delve deeper into the role of neurotransmitters and hormones in this process.

6

Neurotransmitters and Hormones

To further understand how our thoughts and emotions shape our reality, we need to explore the chemical messengers that play vital roles in our brain function: neurotransmitters and hormones. These substances influence our mental states, behaviors, and, ultimately, our ability to manifest our desires.

Introduction to Neurotransmitters and Their Roles in Thought and Emotion

Neurotransmitters are chemicals that transmit signals from one neuron to another across synapses. They are essential for regulating various functions in the brain, including mood, motivation, and cognition. Here are some key neurotransmitters involved in thought and emotion:

Dopamine: Often referred to as the "feel-good" neurotransmitter, dopamine is associated with pleasure, reward, and motivation. It plays a crucial role in reinforcing behaviors and driving us to achieve our goals. High levels of dopamine can enhance focus and drive, making it easier to work towards manifesting our desires.

Serotonin: Serotonin is crucial for regulating mood, sleep, and appetite. It contributes to feelings of well-being and happiness. Adequate levels of serotonin can promote a positive outlook and emotional stability, which are important for maintaining a manifesting mindset.

Norepinephrine: This neurotransmitter is involved in the body's fight-or-flight response. It increases arousal and alertness, preparing the body to respond to stress. While moderate levels can enhance focus and energy, excessive levels can lead to anxiety and stress, hindering manifestation efforts.

GABA (Gamma-Aminobutyric Acid): GABA is an inhibitory neurotransmitter that helps calm the brain and reduce neuronal excitability. It plays a key role in regulating anxiety and promoting relaxation. High levels of GABA can help maintain a calm and focused mind, conducive to effective manifestation practices.

Acetylcholine: Acetylcholine is involved in learning, memory, and attention. It helps facilitate communication between neurons, enhancing cognitive functions that are essential for visualizing and strategizing about our goals.

Impact of Hormones on Brain Function and Behavior

Hormones are chemical messengers that travel through the bloodstream, affecting various bodily functions, including brain activity and behavior. Here are two critical hormones that influence our mental states and manifestation potential:

Cortisol: Known as the "stress hormone," cortisol is released in response to stress and low blood glucose levels. It helps the body manage stress by increasing energy availability and modulating various bodily functions. However, chronic high levels of cortisol can lead to anxiety, depression, and cognitive impairment, all of which can negatively impact our ability to manifest our desires.

Oxytocin: Often called the "love hormone" or "bonding hormone," oxytocin is associated with social bonding, trust, and emotional connection. It promotes feelings of warmth and empathy, enhancing our social interactions and emotional well-being. Positive social interactions and emotional support can boost our confidence and motivation, aiding in the manifestation process.

How Imbalances Can Affect the Mental States and Manifestation Potential

Imbalances in neurotransmitter levels and hormone levels can significantly impact our mental states and, consequently, our manifestation potential:

Dopamine Imbalance:

Low Levels: Can lead to lack of motivation, feelings of apathy, and difficulties in experiencing pleasure, making it challenging to stay focused on manifesting goals.

High Levels: While generally positive, excessively high levels can contribute to risk-taking behaviors and manic episodes, leading to instability.

Serotonin Imbalance:

Low Levels: Associated with depression, anxiety, and mood disorders. These negative emotional states can create mental blocks and reduce the effectiveness of manifestation techniques.

High Levels: Typically beneficial, but extremely high levels (often due to medication) can lead to serotonin syndrome, characterized by confusion and agitation.

Norepinephrine Imbalance:

Low Levels: Can result in lethargy, lack of focus, and difficulty responding to stress, hindering the drive needed for manifestation.

High Levels: Excessive levels can cause chronic stress, anxiety, and an overactive fight-or-flight response, making it hard to maintain a calm and positive mindset.

GABA Imbalance:

Low Levels: Linked to increased anxiety, stress, and insomnia, which can disrupt focus and concentration necessary for manifestation.

High Levels: Generally promote relaxation and calmness, supporting a conducive environment for manifestation.

Cortisol Imbalance:

Chronic High Levels: Lead to persistent stress, impaired cognitive function, and emotional instability, all of which can thwart manifestation efforts.

Low Levels: Can cause fatigue and lack of motivation, reducing the energy available to pursue goals.

Oxytocin Imbalance:

Low Levels: May result in social withdrawal, difficulty forming bonds, and a lack of emotional support, which can undermine the positive emotional states needed for effective manifestation.

High Levels: Generally promote positive social interactions and emotional well-being, enhancing manifestation potential.

By understanding how neurotransmitters and hormones influence our mental states and behaviors, we can better navigate the complex interplay between our thoughts, emotions, and actions. This knowledge empowers us to create an optimal internal environment for manifestation, leveraging the science of the brain to bring our desires into reality.

III

The Energy of Thoughts

7

Electromagnetic Activity

To understand how our thoughts can influence our reality, it's essential to explore the concept of electromagnetic activity in the brain. Our thoughts are not just abstract concepts; they generate measurable electrical and magnetic signals that reflect the brain's activity.

How Brain Activity Generates Electromagnetic Fields?

Our brains are composed of billions of neurons that communicate through electrical impulses. When a neuron fires, it sends an electrical signal down its axon, which then triggers the release of neurotransmitters at the synapse. This process generates tiny electrical currents that create electromagnetic fields.

These electromagnetic fields are the collective result of the synchronized electrical activity of millions of neurons. Although the individual currents are very small, their combined effect produces detectable patterns that can be measured outside the scalp.

Brainwaves and Their Measurement (EEG)

Brainwaves are the rhythmic patterns of electrical activity produced by the brain's neurons. These patterns vary in frequency and amplitude, depending on the brain's state of activity. The primary method for measuring brainwaves is electroencephalography (EEG), a non-invasive technique that involves placing electrodes on the scalp to detect and record the electrical activity of the brain.

Types of Brainwaves: Delta Waves (0.5-4 Hz), Theta Waves (4-8 Hz), Alpha Waves (8-12 Hz), Beta Waves (12-30 Hz), Gamma Waves (30-100 Hz).

How Different States of Consciousness Are Reflected in Brainwave Patterns?

The different brainwave patterns correspond to various states of consciousness, each playing a unique role in our mental and emotional functioning:

Deep Sleep (Delta Waves):

During deep sleep, the brain produces delta waves, which are crucial for physical and mental recovery. This state allows the body to heal and regenerate, and the brain to consolidate memories and process information.

Meditation and Relaxation (Theta and Alpha Waves):

In deep relaxation or meditation, theta and alpha waves become more prominent. These states facilitate access to the subconscious mind, creativity, and deep introspection. They are ideal for visualization and manifesting intentions, as the mind is open and receptive.

Alertness and Focus (Beta Waves):

When we are awake and engaged in cognitive tasks, beta waves dominate. This state is essential for conscious thought, problem-solving, and goal-directed behavior. However, prolonged beta wave activity can lead to stress and anxiety if not balanced with periods of relaxation.

Peak Performance and Insight (Gamma Waves):

Gamma waves are associated with high-level information processing and cognitive functioning. This state is often linked to moments of insight, deep learning, and heightened awareness, making it powerful for achieving breakthroughs and manifesting complex goals.

Understanding these brainwave states and how they correspond to different levels of consciousness can enhance our ability to use manifestation techniques effectively. By intentionally shifting our brainwave patterns through practices like meditation, visualization, and mindfulness, we can create the optimal mental environment for manifesting our desires.

8

Brain Waves

To further grasp the concept of how our thoughts influence our reality, we need to delve into the specifics of brainwaves. These waves represent the electrical activity in the brain and play a crucial role in our cognitive and emotional states. Different brainwaves correspond to different states of consciousness, and understanding them can enhance our ability to manifest our desires.

Different Types of Brainwaves

Delta Waves (0.5-4 Hz): Delta waves are the slowest brainwaves and are most prominent during deep sleep and restorative states. Delta waves are crucial for deep rest and recovery, which are essential for maintaining a balanced mind and body. Adequate deep sleep ensures that the brain and body are rejuvenated, providing the energy and mental clarity needed for effective manifestation.

Theta Waves (4-8 Hz): Theta waves are slower than alpha

waves and occur during light sleep, deep relaxation, and meditation. Theta waves are linked to creativity, intuition, and
the subconscious mind. Theta waves are associated with deep
meditation, creativity, and access to the subconscious mind.
This state is ideal for visualization and reprogramming the
subconscious with positive intentions and goals. Theta waves
enhance creativity and intuition, allowing for powerful insights
and breakthroughs.

Alpha Waves (8-12 Hz): Alpha waves are slower brainwaves
that occur when we are awake but relaxed and not actively
processing information. Alpha waves promote relaxation and
mental coordination. They are often present during meditation,
daydreaming, and light relaxation. This state bridges the
conscious and subconscious mind, which is vital for creative
thinking and manifestation practices. Alpha waves promote
relaxation and mental clarity, making them conducive for
practices like meditation and visualization. Being in an alpha
state allows for a calm, focused mind that can more effectively
concentrate on manifesting desires and goals.

Beta Waves (12-30 Hz): Beta waves are faster brainwaves
that dominate our normal waking state of consciousness when
we are alert, attentive, and engaged in problem-solving or
decision-making. Beta waves are associated with active thinking, focus, and high-level cognitive functioning. While essential for daily tasks and goal achievement, excessive beta
activity can lead to stress and anxiety. Beta waves are essential
for active thinking, planning, and taking action towards goals.
While critical for productivity and goal-directed behavior, it's
important to balance beta activity with relaxation to prevent

stress and burnout, which can hinder manifestation efforts.

Gamma Waves (30-100 Hz): Gamma waves are the fastest brainwaves and are involved in high-level information processing, peak focus, and consciousness. Gamma waves are associated with learning, memory, and information processing. Gamma waves are linked to high-level cognitive processes, including learning, memory, and problem-solving. This state is beneficial for integrating complex ideas and achieving deep insights, supporting the manifestation of more intricate and detailed goals.

Examples of Activities or States That Enhance Specific Brainwaves

Delta Waves: Deep sleep, restorative practices such as yoga nidra, and certain forms of meditation aimed at deep relaxation.

Example: Ensuring a regular sleep schedule and practicing sleep hygiene can enhance delta wave activity, promoting recovery and regeneration.

Theta Waves: Deep meditation, mindfulness practices, creative visualization, and daydreaming.

Example: Engaging in guided meditations that focus on relaxation and visualization can increase theta wave activity, enhancing creativity and intuition.

Alpha Waves: Light meditation, relaxation exercises, and activities that promote a state of calm alertness, such as taking a walk in nature.

Example: Practicing mindfulness or listening to calming music can boost alpha wave activity, helping to bridge the conscious and subconscious mind.

Beta Waves: Focused work, problem-solving tasks, critical thinking, and active learning.

Example: Engaging in puzzles, strategic planning, or any activity that requires active concentration and decision-making can enhance beta wave activity.

Gamma Waves: High-level cognitive tasks, peak performance activities, and certain types of meditation that focus on increasing awareness and consciousness.

Example: Practices like mindfulness meditation, where one maintains a high level of focus and awareness, can increase gamma wave activity, supporting complex problem-solving and integration of new information.

Understanding these brainwave states and their significance allows us to optimize our mental environment for manifestation. By engaging in activities that enhance specific brainwaves, we can cultivate the ideal states of consciousness that support our manifesting efforts. In the next section, we will explore practical techniques for leveraging these brainwave states to enhance our manifestation practices.

9

Measuring Thought Energy

To understand how our thoughts shape our reality, we need tools and techniques to measure the energy of these thoughts. Advances in neuroscience have provided us with various methods to study brain activity and its relationship to our mental states and intentions. Let's explore some of these tools and techniques and how they shed light on the energy of thoughts.

Overview of Tools and Techniques

EEG (Electroencephalography): EEG is a non-invasive technique that measures electrical activity in the brain using electrodes placed on the scalp. EEG records the summed electrical activity of thousands to millions of neurons firing synchronously. It provides real-time information about brainwave patterns and states of consciousness.

fMRI (Functional Magnetic Resonance Imaging): fMRI is a neuroimaging technique that measures changes in blood flow in the brain, which indirectly reflects neural activity. By detecting changes in blood oxygenation levels, fMRI can identify brain regions that are active during specific tasks or mental states. It offers high spatial resolution but lower temporal resolution compared to EEG.

PET (Positron Emission Tomography) and SPECT (Single-Photon Emission Computed Tomography): PET and SPECT are nuclear imaging techniques that measure brain activity by detecting radioactive tracers injected into the bloodstream. These techniques provide information about brain metabolism and neurotransmitter activity. They are less commonly used than EEG and fMRI due to their higher cost and lower temporal resolution.

How These Measurements Provide Insights into the Energy of Thoughts

EEG: EEG allows researchers to observe brainwave patterns associated with different mental states, such as relaxation, meditation, or focused attention. By analyzing these patterns, we can gain insights into the energy of thoughts and how they manifest in the brain. For example, studies have shown that alpha and theta waves increase during meditation and visualization practices, indicating a state of relaxed alertness conducive to manifesting intentions.

fMRI: fMRI provides detailed images of brain activity in response to specific stimuli or tasks. By identifying brain regions involved in thought processes, fMRI helps us understand the neural mechanisms underlying manifestation. For instance, fMRI studies have revealed increased activity in the prefrontal cortex and limbic system during visualization exercises, suggesting that these regions play a role in translating thoughts into actions and emotions.

PET and SPECT: PET and SPECT offer insights into neurotransmitter activity and brain metabolism, providing indirect measures of the energy of thoughts. These techniques help us understand the biochemical basis of mental states and intentions. Research using PET and SPECT has demonstrated changes in dopamine and serotonin levels in response to positive visualization and goal-setting, highlighting the neurochemical basis of manifestation.

Studies That Correlate Brainwave Patterns with Mental States and Intentions

Alpha and Theta Waves in Meditation: Studies using EEG have shown that experienced meditators exhibit increased alpha and theta wave activity during meditation sessions compared to non-meditators. These brainwave patterns are associated with deep relaxation, heightened creativity, and enhanced focus, all of which are conducive to manifesting intentions.

Prefrontal Cortex Activation in Visualization: fMRI studies have demonstrated increased activation in the prefrontal cortex and associated brain regions during visualization exercises. This suggests that the prefrontal cortex plays a role in translating mental imagery into action plans and emotional responses, supporting the manifestation process.

Dopamine Release in Goal-Setting: PET studies have shown that setting and visualizing goals activates reward pathways in the brain, leading to increased dopamine release. This neurotransmitter is associated with motivation, pleasure, and reinforcement learning, indicating that goal-setting can energize thoughts and drive behavior towards desired outcomes.

By combining these neuroimaging techniques with behavioral assessments and subjective reports, researchers can gain a comprehensive understanding of how thoughts influence brain activity and behavior. This interdisciplinary approach helps bridge the gap between subjective experiences and objective measurements, shedding light on the energy of thoughts and its role in manifestation.

IV

Neuroplasticity and Mindset

10

Concept of Neuroplasticity

Neuroplasticity, often referred to as brain plasticity, is the brain's remarkable ability to reorganize and adapt throughout life in response to new experiences, learning, and environmental influences. This concept challenges the long-held belief that the brain's structure and function are fixed after a certain age, highlighting its inherent capacity for change and growth.

Neuroplasticity and Its Importance in Brain Function and Learning

Neuroplasticity refers to the brain's ability to reorganize its structure, functions, and connections in response to internal and external stimuli. It underlies our capacity to learn new skills, form memories, and adapt to changes in our environment. Neuroplasticity is essential for brain development during childhood and continues throughout adulthood, allowing us to acquire knowledge, recover from injuries, and adapt to new challenges.

How the Brain Can Rewire Itself in Response to New Experiences

and Thoughts

The brain's ability to rewire itself is driven by the dynamic nature of its neural networks. When we engage in new experiences or thoughts, neurons form new connections (synapses) or strengthen existing ones through a process called synaptic plasticity. This strengthens the neural pathways associated with the new information or behavior, making it easier for the brain to access and retrieve that information in the future.

Examples of Neuroplasticity in Action, Such as Recovery from Brain Injury

Recovery from Brain Injury: After a traumatic brain injury (TBI), the brain can undergo significant structural and functional changes as part of the recovery process. Through neuroplasticity, undamaged neurons may take on new roles to compensate for lost functions. Rehabilitation programs that focus on repetitive exercises and cognitive tasks can promote neural rewiring and facilitate recovery of lost abilities.

Learning a New Skill: When learning a new skill, such as playing a musical instrument or mastering a language, the brain undergoes structural changes to accommodate the new knowledge. Areas of the brain associated with motor control, language processing, or memory formation may show increased activity and connectivity as a result of learning. With practice, these changes become more pronounced, leading to improved proficiency in the skill.

Adapting to Environmental Changes: In response to changes in our environment, such as moving to a new city or starting a new job, the brain may undergo adaptive changes to optimize its functioning. This may involve reorganizing sensory processing pathways, adjusting emotional responses, or refining decision-making strategies to better suit the new context. Neuroplasticity allows us to adapt to new circumstances and thrive in diverse environments.

By understanding the principles of neuroplasticity, we can harness the brain's inherent capacity for change and growth to cultivate a mindset that fosters personal development and achievement. In the next section, we will explore how mindset influences manifestation and practical techniques for cultivating a mindset conducive to realizing our goals and desires.

11

Growth vs. Fixed Mindset

To fully grasp the interplay between neuroplasticity and manifestation, it's essential to delve into the concept of mindset.
Mindset, a term popularized by psychologist Carol Dweck,
refers to the underlying beliefs we have about learning and
intelligence. Dweck's research highlights two primary types
of mindsets: growth and fixed. Understanding these mindsets
and their impact on our behavior and brain function can significantly enhance our manifestation practices.

Carol Dweck's Research on Growth and Fixed Mindsets

Carol Dweck, a renowned psychologist at Stanford University,
has extensively studied how people's beliefs about their abilities
influence their performance and overall success. According to
Dweck:

Fixed Mindset: Individuals with a fixed mindset believe that
their intelligence, talents, and abilities are static and unchange-
able. They perceive challenges as threats, often avoiding

them for fear of failure. This mindset leads to a desire to appear intelligent rather than actually engaging in learning and growth.

Growth Mindset: Conversely, those with a growth mindset believe that their abilities and intelligence can be developed through effort, learning, and perseverance. They view challenges as opportunities to grow, embrace failures as learning experiences, and persist in the face of setbacks.

How a Growth Mindset Can Foster Positive Changes in the Brain

Adopting a growth mindset can significantly impact neuroplasticity and overall brain function. Here's how:

Increased Neural Connectivity: A growth mindset encourages continuous learning and skill development, promoting the formation of new neural connections. This increased connectivity enhances cognitive flexibility, problem-solving abilities, and creativity.

Enhanced Synaptic Plasticity: Believing in the potential for growth stimulates synaptic plasticity, the process by which synapses (connections between neurons) strengthen with repeated use. This synaptic reinforcement underlies the brain's ability to learn and retain new information.

Resilience and Adaptability: Individuals with a growth mindset are more resilient in the face of challenges. This resilience is reflected in the brain's ability to adapt to new situations and recover from setbacks, further promoting a cycle of growth and learning.

Reduced Stress and Anxiety:A growth mindset reduces the fear of failure, which can alleviate stress and anxiety. Lower stress levels positively impact brain function, particularly in areas related to memory and executive function, enhancing overall mental well-being.

Implications of Mindset on Manifestation Practices

Mindset plays a crucial role in manifestation, as our beliefs and attitudes directly influence our ability to achieve goals and bring desires to fruition. Here's how a growth mindset enhances manifestation practices:

Embracing Challenges: A growth mindset encourages individuals to embrace challenges as opportunities for growth. This perspective is essential for manifestation, as achieving significant goals often requires overcoming obstacles and persisting through difficulties.

Learning from Failure: Viewing failure as a learning experience rather than a setback fosters a proactive approach to goal-setting. This attitude ensures continuous improvement and adaptation, essential for refining manifestation techniques and strategies.

Sustained Effort and Perseverance: Manifestation often requires sustained effort and long-term commitment. A growth mindset reinforces the belief that effort leads to improvement, motivating individuals to persistently work towards their goals, regardless of initial setbacks.

Positive Self-Perception: A growth mindset fosters a positive self-perception, instilling confidence in one's ability to learn and grow. This confidence is crucial for effective manifestation, as believing in one's capacity to achieve goals is a foundational element of the process.

Adaptive Goal-Setting: Individuals with a growth mindset are more likely to set adaptive and flexible goals, adjusting their strategies based on feedback and new information. This adaptability ensures that their manifestation efforts remain aligned with their evolving desires and circumstances.

By cultivating a growth mindset, individuals can enhance their brain's neuroplasticity, fostering an environment conducive to continuous learning and personal development. This mindset not only supports the neurological foundation for manifestation but also empowers individuals to approach their goals with resilience, creativity, and unwavering commitment.

12

Rewiring the Brain

Understanding neuroplasticity and the power of mindset lays a solid foundation for exploring practical techniques to consciously change neural pathways. By adopting specific practices and habits, we can effectively rewire our brains to support positive thinking and manifestation.

Techniques for Consciously Changing Neural Pathways

Repetition: Repetition is a fundamental mechanism for strengthening neural connections. When we repeatedly engage in a thought or behavior, the corresponding neural pathways become more robust, making the thought or behavior more automatic over time. Example: Repeating affirmations daily can reinforce positive beliefs about oneself, gradually shifting the underlying neural circuits associated with self-perception.

Visualization: Visualization involves creating vivid mental images of desired outcomes. This technique activates the same neural networks used when actually experiencing the events, strengthening the neural pathways associated with those out-comes. Example: Visualizing oneself successfully achieving a goal can enhance motivation and confidence, aligning neural activity with the desired outcome.

Mindfulness and Meditation: Mindfulness and meditation practices help to increase awareness of thoughts and emotions, allowing for intentional shifts in focus and perspective. These practices can reduce stress, enhance emotional regulation, and promote positive neural changes. Example: Regular mindful-ness meditation can decrease activity in the amygdala (asso-ciated with stress) and increase connectivity in the prefrontal cortex (associated with executive function).

Positive Self-Talk: Engaging in positive self-talk involves con-sciously replacing negative or limiting thoughts with empow-ering and encouraging ones. This practice helps to reframe the brain's automatic responses to challenges. Example: Instead of thinking, "I can't do this," replacing the thought with, "I can learn to do this with practice," reinforces a growth mindset.

Role of Habits and Sustained Effort in Neural Rewiring

Formation of Habits: Habits are behaviors that become au-tomatic through repeated practice. Forming positive habits involves consistently engaging in desired behaviors until they become ingrained in the brain's neural circuitry. Example: Developing a habit of daily gratitude journaling can enhance overall positivity and well-being by consistently activating neural pathways associated with gratitude and contentment.

Sustained Effort: Neural rewiring requires sustained effort and perseverance. The brain's plasticity means it can change, but meaningful and lasting change often requires continuous and dedicated practice. Example: Committing to a regular exercise routine can improve mental and physical health, but the benefits become more pronounced with consistent effort over time.

Practical Exercises to Begin Rewiring Brains for Positive Thinking

Daily Affirmations:

Exercise: Write down a list of positive affirmations that resonate with your goals and desires. Repeat these affirmations aloud each morning and evening.

Purpose: Reinforces positive beliefs and intentions, strengthening neural pathways associated with these thoughts.

Visualization Practice:

Exercise: Spend 5-10 minutes each day visualizing a specific goal. Imagine every detail vividly, including the emotions you will feel upon achieving it.

Purpose: Activates the neural circuits associated with the desired outcome, aligning your brain's activity with your goals.

Gratitude Journaling:

Exercise: Each night, write down three things you are grateful for. Reflect on why these things matter to you.

Purpose: Shifts focus to positive aspects of life, reinforcing neural pathways linked to gratitude and positivity.

Mindfulness Meditation:

Exercise: Set aside 10-15 minutes daily for mindfulness meditation. Focus on your breath, gently bringing your attention back whenever your mind wanders.

Purpose: Enhances awareness and emotional regulation, promoting positive neural changes.

Positive Self-Talk Challenge:

Exercise: Identify a common negative thought you have. For one week, consciously replace it with a positive alternative whenever it arises.

Purpose: Reframes automatic negative responses, creating new, empowering neural pathways.

By incorporating these techniques into daily routines, individuals can actively participate in the process of neural rewiring, fostering a brain environment conducive to positive thinking and effective manifestation. In the following chapter, we will delve deeper into the science of intention and how to harness it for successful manifestation, building on the foundation of neuroplasticity and mindset.

V

Visualization and the Brain

13

Mechanisms of Visualization

Visualization is a powerful tool that leverages the brain's ability to create vivid mental images of desired outcomes. Understanding the neuroscience behind visualization can enhance our ability to use this technique effectively for manifestation.

Visualization involves the mental rehearsal of specific scenarios or goals, engaging various brain regions in the process. This technique activates neural circuits that mirror the actual experience, making it a potent tool for shaping our reality.

How Visualization Activates Brain Regions Similar to Actual Experiences

Neural Activation: When we visualize an event, the brain's neural activity mirrors that of physically experiencing the event. This phenomenon occurs because the same neural networks are engaged during both real and imagined activities. For example, visualizing running a race activates the motor cortex, the same region involved when we physically run. This neural overlap helps to reinforce the mental imagery, making it more realistic and impactful.

Role of the Visual Cortex and Associative Areas in Creating Mental Images

Visual Cortex: The visual cortex, located in the occipital lobe, is primarily responsible for processing visual information. When we visualize, this area becomes active, similar to when we perceive real visual stimuli. Example: Imagining a vivid sunset can activate the visual cortex, making the mental image as clear and detailed as if we were actually seeing it.

Associative Areas: The associative areas of the brain, including the parietal and temporal lobes, integrate sensory information to create a coherent mental image. These areas help to combine visual details with other sensory inputs, such as sounds or smells, enhancing the richness of the visualization. Example: Visualizing a beach scene might involve not only the image of the waves but also the sound of the ocean and the feeling of sand underfoot, creating a multi-sensory experience in the brain.

Mirror Neurons and Their Function in Visualizing Actions and Outcomes

Mirror Neurons: Mirror neurons are specialized neurons that fire both when we perform an action and when we observe or visualize the same action being performed by others. These neurons are located in areas such as the premotor cortex and the parietal lobe. Mirror neurons play a crucial role in understanding and mimicking others' actions, empathy, and learning new skills through observation. When we visualize ourselves performing a task, mirror neurons help simulate the action, reinforcing the neural pathways needed to execute it. Example: Visualizing oneself successfully delivering a speech can activate mirror neurons, preparing the brain for the actual performance and increasing confidence.

By engaging the visual cortex, associative areas, and mirror neurons, visualization can create a powerful mental rehearsal that enhances performance, builds confidence, and aligns neural activity with desired outcomes. This process makes visualization a vital technique for manifestation, enabling us to mentally experience success before it occurs in reality.

14

Impact on Performance

Visualization's profound impact on performance is well-documented across various fields, from sports to cognitive tasks. This section will review scientific studies demonstrating these effects, provide real-world examples from sports psychology, and explore the placebo effect's role in enhancing the effectiveness of visualization.

Studies Showing How Visualization Improves Physical and Cognitive Performance

Physical Performance

Study Example: A landmark study published in the *Journal of Sport & Exercise Psychology* found that athletes who engaged in mental imagery training showed significant improvements in performance compared to those who did not. The study demonstrated that visualization can enhance motor skills, coordination, and overall physical performance.

Mechanism: Visualization activates the same neural pathways as actual physical practice, reinforcing motor skills and improving muscle memory without physical exertion. This neural priming prepares the body for performance, reducing reaction times and increasing precision.

Cognitive Performance

Study Example: Research published in *Psychological Science* revealed that students who visualized themselves studying effectively and achieving high grades performed better academically than those who did not use visualization techniques. The study highlighted visualization's role in enhancing focus, motivation, and cognitive strategy development.

Mechanism: Visualization fosters a mental rehearsal of cognitive tasks, improving problem-solving skills and enhancing memory retention. It also reduces anxiety and builds confidence, contributing to better academic performance.

Examples from Sports Psychology

Michael Phelps: The Olympic swimmer Michael Phelps famously used visualization as part of his training regimen. Before each race, Phelps would mentally rehearse every stroke, turn, and finish in vivid detail. This practice helped him maintain composure and execute his race strategy flawlessly, contributing to his record-breaking success.

Golf: Professional golfers often use visualization to enhance their performance. By visualizing each shot in detail, including the swing, ball trajectory, and landing, golfers can improve their accuracy and consistency. This technique helps them mentally prepare for various scenarios they might encounter on the course.

Soccer: Soccer players use visualization to improve their skills and strategic thinking. By imagining themselves making successful passes, dribbling around defenders, and scoring goals, players enhance their decision-making abilities and situational awareness during actual matches.

The Placebo Effect and How Belief in Visualization Can Enhance Its Effectiveness

The Placebo Effect

The placebo effect refers to the phenomenon where a person experiences a real improvement in their condition simply because they believe they are receiving an effective treatment, even if the treatment is inactive. This effect highlights the power of belief and expectation in shaping outcomes.

Example: In a study published in the *Journal of Applied Sport Psychology*, athletes who believed in the effectiveness of visualization showed greater performance improvements compared to those who were skeptical. This suggests that the placebo effect can amplify the benefits of visualization by enhancing motivation and confidence.

Enhancing Effectiveness Through Belief

Belief in the power of visualization can significantly enhance its effectiveness. When individuals trust that visualizing their goals and desired outcomes will make a difference, their mental and physiological responses align with that expectation, leading to better results.

Mechanism: Belief in visualization boosts the brain's production of neurotransmitters like dopamine, which are associated with motivation and reward. This positive feedback loop reinforces the neural pathways involved in the visualized actions, making the outcomes more likely to occur.

Practical Implications

To harness the placebo effect, individuals should cultivate a positive mindset and strong belief in their visualization practices. This can be achieved through affirmations, success stories, and regular practice, reinforcing the connection between visualization and successful outcomes.

By understanding and leveraging the mechanisms of visualization and the placebo effect, individuals can significantly enhance their physical and cognitive performance. In the next chapter, we will delve into practical visualization techniques, providing step-by-step guides to help readers integrate these powerful practices into their daily routines, thereby boosting their manifestation potential.

15

Practical Visualization Techniques

To fully harness the power of visualization for enhancing performance and achieving goals, it is essential to practice it effectively. This section provides a step-by-step guide to visualization practices, tips for creating vivid and emotionally charged mental images, and exercises for integrating visualization into daily routines.

Step-by-step Guide to Effective Visualization Practices

Set Clear Intentions

Define Your Goal: Begin by identifying a specific goal or outcome you want to achieve. The more precise and clear your goal, the more effective your visualization will be.

Example: Instead of visualizing general success, focus on a specific scenario like acing a job interview or completing a marathon.

Find a Quiet Space

Minimize Distractions: Choose a quiet, comfortable place where you can relax without interruptions. This helps you focus entirely on your visualization practice.

Example: A peaceful room in your home or a quiet spot in nature.

Relax and Center Yourself

Deep Breathing: Start with a few minutes of deep breathing to calm your mind and body. Inhale slowly through your nose, hold for a few seconds, and exhale through your mouth.

Example: Inhale for a count of four, hold for a count of four, and exhale for a count of four. Repeat this cycle until you feel relaxed.

Create a Vivid Mental Image

Use All Senses: Engage all your senses to create a detailed and vivid mental image of your goal. Imagine the sights, sounds, smells, tastes, and physical sensations associated with achieving your goal.

Example: If visualizing a successful presentation, see the audience's faces, hear the applause, feel the clicker in your hand, and sense the confidence in your body.

Add Emotional Charge

Feel the Emotions: Infuse your visualization with positive emotions such as joy, excitement, and satisfaction. Emotions enhance the neural connections associated with your visualizations.

Example: Feel the pride and happiness of receiving a promotion, the excitement of achieving a personal best time, or the satisfaction of completing a challenging project.

Maintain Consistency

Daily Practice: Dedicate a few minutes each day to your visualization practice. Consistency strengthens the neural pathways associated with your goals.

Example: Set aside 10 minutes every morning or evening for visualization.

Tips for Creating Vivid and Emotionally Charged Mental Images

Use Detailed Descriptions

Be as specific as possible in your mental imagery. The more details you include, the more realistic and impactful the visualization.

Example: Instead of visualizing "being healthy," picture yourself running a 5k race, feeling the breeze on your face, and hearing your feet hit the pavement.

Incorporate Positive Emotions

Emotions are the glue that holds visualizations together. Focus on the positive feelings associated with achieving your goal.

Example: Visualize not just the finish line, but also the exhilaration and pride you'll feel crossing it.

Engage Multiple Senses

Involve as many senses as possible to create a multi-dimensional experience.

Example: If you're visualizing a vacation, imagine the sound of waves, the smell of the ocean, the taste of tropical fruit, and the warmth of the sun.

Exercises for Integrating Visualization into Daily Routines

Morning Visualization Routine: Spend 5-10 minutes each morning visualizing your key goals for the day. Imagine successfully completing tasks and overcoming challenges with ease.

Purpose: Sets a positive tone for the day, preparing your mind for success.

Pre-Sleep Visualization: Before going to sleep, visualize your long-term goals and dreams. Picture yourself living the life you desire, experiencing the emotions and achievements you seek.

Purpose: Embeds positive imagery in your subconscious, influencing your mindset and actions.

Visualization During Breaks: Use short breaks throughout your day to visualize specific aspects of your goals. For instance, before a meeting, visualize it going smoothly and successfully.

Purpose: Reinforces your intentions and maintains focus and motivation throughout the day.

Incorporate Movement: Pair visualization with physical movement, such as walking or gentle stretching. This can enhance the sensory experience and make the visualization more dynamic.

Purpose: Engages both mind and body, creating a holistic approach to visualization.

Visualization Journal: Keep a journal where you write down your visualizations in detail. Include descriptions of the images, emotions, and sensations you experienced.

Purpose: Reinforces visualizations through writing, making them more concrete and memorable.

By incorporating these practical visualization techniques into daily routines, individuals can effectively harness the power of their brains to achieve their goals and enhance their overall well-being. In the next chapter, we will explore the science of intention and how to align it with visualization practices for optimal manifestation results.

VI

The Mind-Body Connection

16

Psychosomatic Effects

Understanding the mind-body connection is crucial for comprehending how thoughts and emotions can manifest into physical realities. This chapter delves into the psychosomatic effects, exploring the intricate relationship between mind and body, and providing scientific evidence to support these concepts.

The term "psychosomatic" refers to the connection between the mind (psyche) and the body (soma). Psychosomatic effects occur when psychological factors like thoughts, emotions, and beliefs lead to physical changes in the body. This relationship is fundamental in understanding how our mental state can influence our physical health.

Relationship Between Mind and Body in Influencing Health

Stress and Physical Health: Chronic stress is a prime example of how mental states can affect physical health. When the brain perceives a threat, it triggers the release of stress hormones like cortisol and adrenaline. While these hormones are essential for acute stress responses, prolonged exposure can lead to adverse health effects.

Example: Persistent high cortisol levels can suppress the immune system, increase blood pressure, and contribute to the development of conditions such as hypertension, diabetes, and cardiovascular diseases.

Placebo and Nocebo Effects: The placebo effect occurs when patients experience real improvements in their health after receiving a treatment that has no therapeutic value, simply because they believe it will work. Conversely, the nocebo effect happens when negative expectations of a treatment cause adverse effects.

Example: Studies have shown that patients taking a placebo for pain relief often report significant reductions in pain, highlighting the power of belief and expectation in physical health outcomes.

Emotional Well-being and Immune Function: Positive emotions and mental states, such as happiness and optimism, can enhance immune function. Conversely, negative emotions like depression and anxiety can impair it.

Example: Research has demonstrated that individuals with a positive outlook have a stronger immune response to vaccines compared to those with a negative outlook.

How Thoughts and Emotions Can Lead to Physical Changes

Psychoneuroimmunology (PNI): PNI is the study of how psychological processes, the nervous system, and the immune system interact. This field provides insights into how stress and emotions can influence immune function and overall health.

Example: Studies in PNI have shown that chronic stress can lead to increased susceptibility to infections and slower wound healing, illustrating the impact of psychological states on physical health.

Cardiovascular Health: Emotions like anger, anxiety, and sadness can have a direct impact on cardiovascular health. These emotions can lead to increased heart rate, blood pressure, and vascular resistance, which over time, can contribute to heart disease.

Example: Research has found that individuals who frequently experience anger and hostility are at a higher risk of developing coronary heart disease.

Gut-Brain Axis: The gut-brain axis refers to the bidirectional communication between the gut and the brain. This connection explains how mental states can influence gastrointestinal health and vice versa.

Example: Stress and anxiety can exacerbate conditions like irritable bowel syndrome (IBS), demonstrating the interplay between emotional and digestive health.

Scientific Evidence Supporting the Mind-Body Connection

Harvard Study on Relaxation Response: A study conducted by Harvard Medical School investigated the "relaxation response," a state of deep rest induced by practices like meditation and deep breathing. The study found that individuals who regularly elicited the relaxation response had lower blood pressure, reduced heart rate, and enhanced immune function.

Conclusion: The findings support the idea that mental practices can lead to measurable physical health benefits.

Yale Study on Optimism and Heart Health: Researchers at Yale University found that older adults with positive attitudes about aging lived longer and had a lower risk of heart disease compared to those with negative attitudes.

Conclusion: The study highlights the powerful role of mental outlook in influencing longevity and cardiovascular health.

University of Wisconsin Study on Meditation and Immune Function: A study by the University of Wisconsin-Madison examined the effects of mindfulness meditation on immune function. Participants who underwent an eight-week mindfulness meditation program showed significant increases in antibody production in response to a flu vaccine.

Conclusion: The research provides evidence that mental practices like meditation can enhance immune response, illustrating the mind–body connection.

Understanding the mind–body connection underscores the importance of maintaining a positive mental state for physical health and well-being. In the next section, we will explore techniques to enhance this connection, providing readers with practical tools to improve both mental and physical health through the power of positive thinking and emotional regulation.

17

Placebo Effect

The placebo effect is a fascinating phenomenon that under-scores the powerful interplay between the mind and body. This section explains the placebo effect, its neurological basis, and how belief and expectation can lead to real physiological changes. Additionally, it presents studies demonstrating the power of the placebo effect.

Placebo Effect and Its Neurological Basis

Definition of the Placebo Effect: The placebo effect occurs when a person experiences a real improvement in their con-dition after receiving a treatment that has no therapeutic value. This improvement is driven by the individual's belief and expectation that the treatment will work.

Example: A sugar pill given to patients as a painkiller can lead to a significant reduction in pain if the patients believe it is a real medication.

Neurological Basis: Brain Regions Involved: The placebo effect engages various brain regions, including the prefrontal cortex, which is involved in expectation and planning, and the anterior cingulate cortex, which processes pain and emotion.

Neurotransmitters: The release of neurotransmitters such as dopamine and endorphins is crucial in mediating the placebo effect. These chemicals are associated with feelings of reward and pain relief.

Mechanism: When a person believes a treatment will work, the brain anticipates a positive outcome and releases these neurotransmitters, leading to real physiological changes. This can result in reduced pain, improved mood, and enhanced overall health.

How Belief and Expectation Can Lead to Real Physiological Changes

Expectation and Pain Reduction: Belief in a treatment can activate the brain's pain relief pathways, leading to the release of endorphins, which are natural painkillers. This can result in significant pain reduction, even if the treatment itself is inert.

Example: Patients with chronic pain who believe they are receiving a potent painkiller may experience substantial pain relief, even if the treatment is a placebo.

Psychological Mechanisms: Confidence and Self-Efficacy: Belief in the effectiveness of a treatment can boost confidence and self-efficacy, leading to better health outcomes. This psychological boost can enhance motivation, adherence to treatment, and overall well-being.

Example: A patient with depression may experience improved mood and energy levels if they believe their therapy or medication will be effective, even if it is a placebo.

Physiological Responses: Immune System Modulation: Expectation and belief can influence the immune system. Studies have shown that positive expectations can enhance immune response, while negative expectations can suppress it.

Example: Patients who believe in the effectiveness of a placebo treatment for a cold may exhibit a stronger immune response and faster recovery.

Studies That Demonstrate the Power of the Placebo Effect

Pain Management

Study: A study published in *The Lancet* investigated the placebo effect in patients with chronic pain. Participants were given either a placebo pill or no treatment at all. Those who received the placebo reported a significant reduction in pain compared to the control group.

Conclusion: The study highlighted the powerful role of expectation and belief in pain management, demonstrating that placebo treatments can trigger real pain relief.

Parkinson's Disease

Study: Research published in *Nature Neuroscience* explored the placebo effect in patients with Parkinson's disease. Patients who believed they were receiving an active treatment showed increased dopamine release in the brain, resulting in improved motor function.

Conclusion: The study provided evidence that the placebo effect can lead to measurable changes in brain chemistry, improving symptoms in neurological conditions.

Depression

Study: A meta-analysis published in *JAMA Psychiatry* examined the placebo effect in clinical trials for antidepressants. The analysis found that a significant portion of the therapeutic response to antidepressants could be attributed to placebo effects.

Conclusion: The study underscored the importance of belief and expectation in treating mental health conditions, highlighting the placebo effect's potential to enhance treatment outcomes.

By understanding the placebo effect and its neurological basis, we can appreciate the profound impact that belief and expectation have on our health. This knowledge can be harnessed to improve therapeutic outcomes and enhance the efficacy of various treatments. In the next section, we will explore practical techniques for leveraging the mind-body connection to promote health and well-being, building on the principles discussed in this chapter.

18

Stress and Relaxation Responses

Understanding the brain's response to stress and how we can actively manage and mitigate stress through relaxation techniques is crucial for maintaining overall health. This section will explain the brain's response to stress, discuss the role of the autonomic nervous system, and provide practical techniques for managing stress and promoting relaxation.

Brain's Response to Stress (Fight or Flight Response)

The Fight or Flight Response

When faced with a perceived threat, the brain initiates the fight or flight response to prepare the body for immediate action. This response is primarily managed by the amygdala, which processes emotional reactions and signals danger.

Activation of the Hypothalamus: Upon recognizing a threat, the amygdala sends a distress signal to the hypothalamus, which acts as the command center of the brain.

Release of Stress Hormones: The hypothalamus activates the sympathetic nervous system, prompting the adrenal glands to release adrenaline and cortisol. These stress hormones increase heart rate, blood pressure, and energy supplies, preparing the body to either fight or flee from the threat.

Physical Manifestations: Physiological changes include dilated pupils, increased respiration rate, tensed muscles, and heightened senses, all designed to optimize the body for immediate physical activity.

Chronic Stress

While the fight or flight response is beneficial in short-term, acute situations, chronic activation due to ongoing stress can lead to various health issues, including anxiety, depression, cardiovascular disease, and weakened immune function.

Example: Prolonged exposure to stressors such as work pressure, financial difficulties, or personal conflicts can keep the body in a constant state of alert, leading to detrimental health effects.

Role of the Autonomic Nervous System in Stress and Relaxation

Autonomic Nervous System (ANS): The ANS controls involuntary bodily functions, including heart rate, digestion, respiratory rate, and reflexes. It comprises two main branches: the sympathetic nervous system (SNS) and the parasympathetic nervous system (PNS).

Sympathetic Nervous System (SNS): The SNS is responsible for the fight or flight response. It prepares the body for action by increasing heart rate, redirecting blood flow to muscles, and releasing energy stores.

Activation: The SNS is activated by stressors, both physical and psychological, triggering the release of adrenaline and cortisol.

Parasympathetic Nervous System (PNS): The PNS promotes the rest and digest response, helping the body to relax and recover after the threat has passed. It slows the heart rate, promotes digestion, and conserves energy.

Relaxation Response: Activation of the PNS counteracts the effects of the SNS, bringing the body back to a state of calm and balance.

Techniques for Managing Stress and Promoting Relaxation

Mindfulness Meditation: Mindfulness meditation involves focusing on the present moment and accepting it without judgment. This practice helps reduce stress by calming the mind and enhancing self-awareness.

Technique: Find a quiet space, sit comfortably, and focus on your breath. Notice the sensations of each inhale and exhale. When your mind wanders, gently bring your attention back to your breath.

Benefits: Reduces anxiety, lowers cortisol levels, and improves emotional regulation.

Deep Breathing Exercises: Deep breathing activates the PNS, promoting relaxation and reducing the physiological effects of stress.

Technique: Practice diaphragmatic breathing by inhaling deeply through your nose, allowing your abdomen to expand, holding for a few seconds, and exhaling slowly through your mouth.

Example: The 4-7-8 technique—inhale for 4 seconds, hold for 7 seconds, exhale for 8 seconds.

Benefits: Lowers heart rate, reduces blood pressure, and calms the nervous system.

Progressive Muscle Relaxation (PMR): PMR involves tensing and then relaxing different muscle groups to release physical tension and promote relaxation.

Technique: Start at your feet and work your way up, tensing each muscle group for 5-10 seconds and then relaxing for 15-20 seconds.

Benefits: Reduces muscle tension, lowers stress levels, and promotes a sense of physical relaxation.

Guided Imagery: Guided imagery involves visualizing peaceful and calming scenes to reduce stress and promote relaxation.

Technique: Close your eyes and imagine a serene place, such as a beach or forest. Engage all your senses to make the scene as vivid as possible, imagining the sights, sounds, smells, and feelings of being in that place.

Benefits: Enhances relaxation, reduces stress, and improves mental well-being.

Exercise: Physical activity helps reduce stress hormones and stimulates the production of endorphins, which are natural mood lifters.

Technique: Incorporate regular exercise into your routine, such as walking, jogging, yoga, or any physical activity you enjoy.

Benefits: Improves physical health, reduces anxiety, and enhances overall mood.

By understanding the brain's response to stress and utilizing these relaxation techniques, individuals can effectively manage stress and promote a state of calm and well-being. In the next chapter, we will explore the concept of intention and how aligning it with visualization and relaxation practices can enhance manifestation potential.

VII

The Power of Belief and Intention

19

Role of Belief Systems

Belief and intention are fundamental to the process of manifestation. This chapter explores how belief systems are formed, their influence on perception and behavior, the neurological basis of belief, and how changing beliefs can lead to different outcomes.

Formation of Beliefs

Early Influences: Beliefs are typically formed early in life through interactions with family, culture, and experiences. These early influences shape our understanding of the world and our place in it.

Cognitive Frameworks: As we grow, our beliefs form cognitive frameworks or mental models that help us interpret and navigate the world. These frameworks are reinforced through repetition and experiences.

Example: A child repeatedly told they are intelligent is likely to develop a strong belief in their intellectual abilities, influencing their academic performance and confidence.

Influence on Perception and Behavior

Perception: Beliefs act as filters through which we perceive reality. They influence what we notice, how we interpret events, and how we react to situations.

Behavior: Beliefs drive behavior by shaping our goals, motivations, and actions. Positive beliefs can lead to proactive behavior, while negative beliefs can result in avoidance or self-sabotage.

Example: Someone who believes they are capable of achieving their goals is more likely to take risks and persist in the face of challenges, leading to greater success.

Neurological Basis of Belief and Its Impact on Neural Pathways

Neurological Basis of Belief

Brain Regions: The prefrontal cortex (involved in decision-making and reasoning) and the limbic system (involved in emotions) play key roles in the formation and reinforcement of beliefs.

Neural Pathways: Beliefs are encoded in neural pathways, which are strengthened through repeated thought patterns and experiences. The more a belief is reinforced, the stronger the associated neural pathway becomes.

Impact on Neural Pathways

Neural Plasticity: The brain's ability to rewire itself, known as neuroplasticity, allows for the possibility of changing beliefs. When new beliefs are formed and practiced, new neural pathways are created and old ones can weaken.

Example: If someone consciously shifts their belief from "I am not good enough" to "I am capable and deserving," over time, the new belief can become the dominant neural pathway, influencing their behavior and experiences.

Beliefs and Cognitive Dissonance

Cognitive Dissonance: When new information conflicts with existing beliefs, it creates cognitive dissonance, an uncomfortable state that the brain seeks to resolve. This can lead to a re-evaluation and potential change in beliefs.

Example: If a person who believes they are not creative receives consistent positive feedback on their creative work, they may eventually adjust their belief to align with this new evidence.

How Changing Beliefs Can Lead to Different Outcomes

Shifting Limiting Beliefs

Identification: The first step in changing beliefs is identifying limiting beliefs that hinder progress. This can be done through self-reflection, feedback, and recognizing patterns of thought and behavior.

Reframing: Once identified, limiting beliefs can be reframed into empowering beliefs. This involves consciously challenging and replacing negative thought patterns with positive affirmations and evidence-based perspectives.

Example: Reframing "I can't do this" to "I am learning and growing every day" can shift one's approach to challenges, leading to greater persistence and resilience.

Impact on Outcomes

Behavioral Change: Changing beliefs leads to changes in behavior. Empowering beliefs encourage proactive behavior, risk-taking, and perseverance, while limiting beliefs often result in avoidance and self-doubt.

Emotional Well-being: Positive beliefs contribute to improved emotional well-being by reducing stress, anxiety, and negative self-talk. This can enhance overall mental health and life satisfaction.

Example: Believing in one's ability to succeed can lead to setting higher goals, pursuing opportunities, and achieving greater success in personal and professional endeavors.

Neuro-Linguistic Programming (NLP)

Techniques: NLP offers techniques for changing beliefs through language and thought patterns. Techniques such as visualization, affirmations, and anchoring can help reprogram the mind to support new, positive beliefs.

Example: Visualizing a successful outcome and repeatedly affirming one's capability can reinforce new beliefs, creating a positive feedback loop that influences behavior and results.

Self-Fulfilling Prophecies

Concept: A self-fulfilling prophecy occurs when a belief leads to actions that cause the belief to come true. Positive beliefs can create a cycle of success, while negative beliefs can perpetuate failure.

Example: A student who believes they are good at math is likely to study more, seek help when needed, and perform well, reinforcing their belief. Conversely, a student who believes they are bad at math may avoid studying, leading to poor performance and reinforcing their negative belief.

By understanding the power of belief and intention, individuals can harness these principles to create positive changes in their lives. The next chapter will explore the practical application of these concepts, providing tools and techniques for cultivating empowering beliefs and aligning intentions with desired outcomes.

20

Intention Setting

Setting clear and purposeful intentions is a powerful practice that can shape our thoughts, behaviors, and ultimately our reality. This section delves into the neuroscience behind intention setting, provides practical steps for setting and maintaining clear intentions, and explains how intention can influence outcomes.

Neuroscience Behind Setting Intentions and Their Impact on Brain Function

The Role of the Prefrontal Cortex: The prefrontal cortex is critical for planning, decision-making, and setting goals. When we set an intention, this brain region is activated, helping to create a clear plan and directing our attention towards achieving that goal.

Example: Setting an intention to exercise regularly activates the prefrontal cortex, which then helps to organize daily activities to accommodate workout sessions.

The Reticular Activating System (RAS): The RAS is a network of neurons located in the brainstem that plays a crucial role in attention and awareness. When we set an intention, the RAS filters information, allowing us to focus on relevant stimuli that align with our goals.

Example: If you set an intention to find opportunities for career growth, the RAS will make you more aware of job openings, networking events, and other opportunities that you might have otherwise overlooked.

Neuroplasticity and Intention: Intentions, when repeated and reinforced, can lead to changes in neural pathways through the process of neuroplasticity. Consistently focusing on a specific intention strengthens the neural circuits associated with the behaviors and actions needed to achieve it.

Example: Regularly setting an intention to practice gratitude can rewire the brain to more easily recognize and appreciate positive aspects of life, enhancing overall well-being.

Practical Steps for Setting and Maintaining Clear Intentions

Clarity and Specificity

Define Your Intention: Be clear and specific about what you want to achieve. Vague intentions lead to vague results.

Example: Instead of setting an intention to "be healthier," specify actions such as "exercise for 30 minutes every day" or "eat five servings of vegetables daily."

Visualization

Create a Mental Image: Visualize the outcome of your intention as vividly as possible. This engages the brain's visual and associative regions, making the intention more tangible and real.

Example: If your intention is to run a marathon, visualize yourself crossing the finish line, feeling strong and accomplished.

Affirmations

Positive Statements: Use affirmations to reinforce your intentions. Repeat positive, present-tense statements that align with your goals.

Example: "I am confident and capable of achieving my goals" can reinforce a positive mindset and motivate action.

Emotional Engagement

Connect with Emotion: Attach positive emotions to your intentions. Emotions strengthen the neural pathways associated with your intentions, making them more compelling and motivating.

Example: Feel the excitement and pride of achieving your goal, whether it's completing a project, learning a new skill, or improving a relationship.

Consistency

Daily Practice: Revisit and reinforce your intentions daily. Consistency helps to engrain the intention in your neural circuitry.

Example: Spend a few minutes each morning and evening reflecting on your intentions, visualizing success, and repeating affirmations.

Accountability

Track Progress: Keep a journal or use a digital tracker to monitor your progress. Reflecting on your achievements and challenges helps to maintain focus and motivation.

Example: Write down your daily actions that align with your intentions and review them weekly to assess progress and make adjustments.

How Intention Can Influence Outcomes

Focused Attention

Enhanced Awareness: Setting an intention directs your brain's focus towards relevant opportunities and resources that can help you achieve your goal.

Example: An intention to improve public speaking skills might lead you to notice and attend workshops, seek feedback, and practice more frequently.

Behavioral Alignment

Consistent Actions: Intentions influence your daily actions and decisions, aligning your behavior with your goals. This consistent alignment increases the likelihood of achieving desired outcomes.

Example: Setting an intention to save money will likely lead you to make more mindful spending decisions, find ways to increase income, and create a budget.

Positive Feedback Loop

Reinforcement: Achieving small milestones related to your intention reinforces the belief in your ability to succeed, creating a positive feedback loop that fuels further progress.

Example: Successfully completing a 5K run as part of a larger goal to improve fitness can boost confidence and motivation to continue training for longer races.

Resilience and Adaptability

Overcoming Obstacles: Clear intentions provide a sense of purpose and direction, helping you to stay resilient in the face of challenges and adaptable to changing circumstances.

Example: When faced with setbacks, such as a project delay, a clear intention helps you to stay focused on the end goal and find alternative paths to achieve it.

By understanding and applying the principles of intention setting, individuals can harness the power of their minds to create positive changes and achieve their goals. The next chapter will explore the practical application of these concepts in daily life, offering tools and strategies for cultivating empowering beliefs, setting clear intentions, and aligning actions with desired outcomes.

21

Research on Intention

Understanding the scientific basis for the power of intention involves reviewing studies that examine how focused thought, meditation, prayer, and other intention-based practices affect the brain and behavior. This section presents key findings from relevant research and discusses their implications for personal manifestation practices.

Scientific Studies on the Power of Intention and Focused Thought

Intention and Brain Activity

Study Example: A study conducted by the University of Wisconsin-Madison found that individuals who practiced loving-kindness meditation showed increased activity in the prefrontal cortex, a region associated with goal-setting and intention.

Findings: The results indicate that focusing on positive intentions can enhance brain regions involved in planning and executing actions aligned with those intentions.

Mindfulness and Neuroplasticity

Study Example: Research from Harvard Medical School demonstrated that regular mindfulness meditation could increase gray matter density in the hippocampus (involved in learning and memory) and reduce gray matter density in the amygdala (involved in stress and anxiety).

Findings: These changes suggest that intention-based practices like mindfulness can physically alter brain structures, enhancing cognitive functions and emotional regulation.

The Placebo Effect and Intention

Study Example: A meta-analysis published in the Journal of Clinical Psychology explored the placebo effect, showing that patients' expectations and beliefs (a form of intention) could significantly influence their health outcomes.

Findings: The power of belief and focused intention can produce measurable physiological changes, supporting the idea that our thoughts and intentions can directly impact our well-being.

Findings from Research on Meditation, Prayer, and Other Intention-Based Practices

Meditation

Study Example: A study by the Massachusetts General Hospital found that individuals who practiced meditation for eight weeks showed measurable changes in brain regions associated with memory, sense of self, empathy, and stress.

Findings: The practice of meditation, which involves setting intentions and focusing thought, can lead to structural brain changes that enhance mental and emotional health.

Prayer

Study Example: Research published in the Journal of Behavioral Medicine examined the effects of intercessory prayer on patients undergoing heart surgery. While results varied, some studies indicated that patients who knew they were being prayed for experienced better recovery outcomes.

Findings: The act of prayer, which involves setting a focused intention for another's well-being, can have psychological and sometimes physiological effects, suggesting a potential mechanism by which intention influences outcomes.

Visualization

Study Example: Research on athletes has shown that visualization practices can improve physical performance. A study published in the Journal of Sport and Exercise Psychology found that athletes who regularly visualized their performance improved their skills more than those who did not.

Findings: Visualization, a practice that involves setting clear intentions and mentally rehearsing outcomes, can enhance physical abilities and performance, indicating that the brain cannot always distinguish between imagined and real experiences.

Implications of These Studies for Personal Manifestation Practices

Enhancing Mental Focus

Implication: By understanding that focused thought and intention can physically alter brain structures and functions, individuals can leverage practices like meditation and visualization to enhance mental focus and clarity.

Application: Incorporate regular meditation sessions into your routine to strengthen the prefrontal cortex and improve your ability to set and achieve intentions.

Promoting Emotional Well-being

Implication: Intention-based practices can reduce stress and improve emotional regulation, contributing to overall well-being.

Application: Use loving-kindness meditation or gratitude practices to cultivate positive emotions and reduce anxiety, creating a more conducive mental environment for manifestation.

Improving Physical Health

Implication: The placebo effect and studies on prayer suggest that belief and intention can influence physical health outcomes.

Application: Set positive health intentions and engage in practices like visualization or prayer to support physical healing and well-being.

Boosting Performance and Achievement

Implication: Visualization and focused intention can enhance performance in various areas, from sports to academics and career pursuits.

Application: Regularly visualize your goals and the steps needed to achieve them, enhancing your motivation and performance through mental rehearsal.

Creating Positive Belief Systems

Implication: Understanding that beliefs shape neural pathways highlights the importance of cultivating positive, empowering beliefs.

Application: Identify and reframe limiting beliefs, using affirmations and visualizations to establish new, supportive neural pathways that align with your intentions.

By integrating these research-backed practices into daily life, individuals can harness the power of intention to manifest desired outcomes more effectively. The next chapter will explore the practical application of these concepts, providing tools and strategies for cultivating empowering beliefs, setting clear intentions, and aligning actions with desired outcomes.

VIII

Emotional Regulation and Manifestation

22

Amygdala and Emotional Processing

Emotional regulation plays a crucial role in the process of manifestation. Understanding how the brain processes emotions and learning techniques to manage them can significantly influence our ability to manifest desired outcomes. This chapter focuses on the amygdala's role in emotional processing, how emotional regulation affects brain function and behavior, and provides practical techniques for managing emotions.

Role of the Amygdala

Emotional Hub: The amygdala, an almond-shaped set of neurons located deep within the brain's temporal lobes, is central to processing emotions, particularly fear and pleasure.

Fight or Flight Response: When faced with a threat, the amygdala triggers the fight-or-flight response, releasing stress hormones like cortisol and adrenaline. This response prepares the body to react quickly to danger.

Memory and Learning: The amygdala is also involved in forming emotional memories. Strong emotional experiences, whether positive or negative, are more likely to be remembered because the amygdala enhances the encoding of these memories.

Emotional Regulation and Its Influence on the Brain and Behavior

Impact on Prefrontal Cortex: The prefrontal cortex, which is responsible for executive functions like decision-making and impulse control, interacts with the amygdala. Effective emotional regulation can enhance the functioning of the prefrontal cortex, leading to better decision-making and goal-setting.

Behavioral Consequences: Poor emotional regulation can result in impulsive actions, stress-related behaviors, and difficulties in achieving long-term goals. Conversely, good emotional regulation can improve focus, resilience, and the ability to pursue and achieve intentions.

Techniques for Managing Negative Emotions and Enhancing Positive Ones

Mindfulness Meditation

Technique: Mindfulness involves paying attention to the present moment without judgment. It helps increase awareness of emotional states and reduces reactivity to negative emotions.

Practice: Spend 10-20 minutes daily in a quiet space, focusing on your breath and observing your thoughts and emotions as they arise. Let go of judgments and simply notice your feelings.

Cognitive Reappraisal

Technique: Cognitive reappraisal involves changing the way you think about a situation to alter its emotional impact. It helps in reducing negative emotions and promoting a more positive outlook.

Practice: When faced with a stressful situation, try to identify and challenge negative thoughts. Reframe the situation by finding alternative, more positive interpretations.

Gratitude Practice

Technique: Regularly practicing gratitude can enhance positive emotions and reduce stress. Focusing on what you are thankful for shifts attention away from negative emotions and fosters a sense of well-being.

Practice: Keep a gratitude journal and write down three things you are grateful for each day. Reflect on these positive aspects of your life to cultivate a more positive mindset.

Breathing Exercises

Technique: Deep breathing exercises activate the parasympathetic nervous system, promoting relaxation and reducing the stress response.

Practice: Practice deep breathing by inhaling slowly through your nose for a count of four, holding your breath for a count of four, and exhaling through your mouth for a count of six. Repeat this cycle for several minutes, especially during moments of stress.

Physical Exercise

Technique: Regular physical activity releases endorphins, which are natural mood lifters. Exercise also helps reduce levels of cortisol, the stress hormone.

Practice: Engage in moderate to vigorous physical activity for at least 30 minutes most days of the week. Activities like walking, running, yoga, or dancing can significantly improve mood and emotional regulation.

Positive Visualization

Technique: Visualization involves imagining positive outcomes and experiences. This practice can enhance positive emotions and increase motivation.

Practice: Spend a few minutes each day visualizing a positive future. Imagine achieving your goals and experiencing joy, success, and fulfillment. Focus on the sensory details and emotions associated with these positive scenarios.

Social Support

Technique: Building and maintaining strong social connections can provide emotional support and reduce feelings of stress and loneliness.

Practice: Spend time with friends and family, participate in social activities, and seek support from loved ones during challenging times. Sharing your feelings with a trusted person can help you process and regulate emotions.

By incorporating these techniques into daily life, individuals can better manage their emotions, creating a mental environment conducive to successful manifestation. Effective emotional regulation enhances focus, resilience, and overall well-being, making it easier to align thoughts and actions with intentions. The next chapter will explore the practical application of these concepts, offering strategies for integrating emotional regula-tion practices into a manifestation routine.

23

Techniques for Emotional Control

Effective emotional control is essential for maintaining mental well-being and facilitating the manifestation process. This section introduces methods such as mindfulness, meditation, and cognitive-behavioral therapy (CBT) for managing emotions. We will discuss the neurological effects of these practices on emotional regulation and provide exercises for readers to practice emotional control and resilience.

Introduction to Methods

Mindfulness: Mindfulness involves paying attention to the present moment with openness, curiosity, and acceptance. It helps individuals become aware of their thoughts, feelings, and bodily sensations without judgment.

Meditation: Meditation practices vary but generally involve focusing attention on a specific object, thought, or activity to cultivate mental clarity, emotional balance, and relaxation.

Cognitive-Behavioral Therapy (CBT): CBT is a psychotherapeutic approach that focuses on identifying and challenging negative thought patterns and behaviors. It helps individuals develop healthier ways of thinking and responding to emotional triggers.

Neurological Effects on Emotional Regulation

Mindfulness and Meditation: Research shows that mindfulness and meditation practices can lead to structural and functional changes in the brain, particularly in areas associated with emotion regulation.

Regular practice of mindfulness and meditation strengthens connections between the prefrontal cortex (responsible for executive functions) and the amygdala (involved in emotional processing), leading to better regulation of emotional responses.

Cognitive-Behavioral Therapy (CBT): CBT has been found to alter brain activity and connectivity patterns associated with emotional regulation. It helps individuals develop adaptive coping strategies and reframe negative thought patterns, leading to more effective emotional control.

Studies using neuroimaging techniques have shown changes in brain activity in regions such as the prefrontal cortex and anterior cingulate cortex following CBT interventions.

Exercises for Practicing Emotional Control and Resilience

Mindful Breathing

- Sit comfortably and focus your attention on your breath.

- Notice the sensations of each inhale and exhale, without trying to change anything.
- Whenever your mind wanders, gently bring your focus back to your breath.
- Practice for 5-10 minutes daily to develop mindfulness and enhance emotional regulation.

Body Scan Meditation

- Lie down or sit comfortably with your eyes closed.
- Starting from your toes, gradually shift your attention through each part of your body, noticing any sensations without judgment.
- Pay attention to areas of tension or discomfort, and breathe into those areas, allowing them to relax.
- Continue scanning your entire body, from toes to head, and back down again.
- Practice for 10-20 minutes to release physical tension and promote emotional relaxation.

CBT Thought Record

- Identify a negative thought or belief that is causing distress.
- Write down the situation or trigger that led to the negative thought.
- Identify the automatic thought that arose in response to the situation.
- Challenge the automatic thought by considering alternative perspectives or evidence.
- Replace the negative thought with a more balanced or positive alternative.

- Repeat this process whenever you notice unhelpful thought patterns, gradually reshaping your cognitive responses.

Gratitude Journaling

- Take a few minutes each day to write down three things you are grateful for.
- Reflect on the positive aspects of your life, no matter how small or seemingly insignificant.
- Cultivate a mindset of gratitude and appreciation, shifting your focus away from negative emotions towards positive experiences.

Progressive Muscle Relaxation (PMR)

- Tense each muscle group in your body for 5-10 seconds, starting from your toes and working your way up to your head.
- Release the tension and allow the muscles to relax completely for 15-20 seconds.
- Notice the difference between tension and relaxation in each muscle group.
- Practice PMR regularly to reduce physical tension and promote emotional calmness.

By incorporating these exercises into your daily routine, you can develop greater emotional control and resilience, enabling you to manage stress, regulate emotions, and maintain a positive mindset. These practices support the manifestation process by creating an internal environment conducive to aligning thoughts and actions with intentions.

24

Impact on Manifestation

Emotional states play a significant role in the manifestation process, influencing our ability to attract and create desired outcomes. This section explores how emotional regulation directly affects manifestation, the role of positive emotions in enhancing neural connectivity and manifestation potential, and provides examples of successful manifestation through effective emotional regulation.

How Emotional States Affect the Ability to Manifest Desired Outcomes

Vibrational Alignment: Emotions emit vibrational frequencies that resonate with similar frequencies in the universe. Positive emotions such as joy, gratitude, and love vibrate at higher frequencies, aligning with positive outcomes.

Negative emotions like fear, doubt, and anger vibrate at lower frequencies and can hinder manifestation by attracting undesired outcomes or blocking the flow of abundance.

Law of Attraction: The Law of Attraction posits that like attracts like meaning the emotions we predominantly feel and express attract corresponding experiences into our lives.

When we are in a state of alignment with our desires, characterized by positive emotions and beliefs, we become magnetic to opportunities and resources that support the realization of those desires.

Role of Positive Emotions in Enhancing Neural Connectivity and Manifestation Potential

Neural Connectivity and Positive Emotions: Positive emotions stimulate the release of neurotransmitters such as dopamine, serotonin, and endorphins, which promote feelings of happiness, well-being, and satisfaction.

These neurotransmitters enhance neural connectivity in the brain, facilitating clearer thinking, creativity, and problem-solving abilities, all of which are essential for effective manifestation.

Optimism and Manifestation Potential: Optimism, a positive emotional state characterized by hopeful and confident attitudes, is associated with resilience, persistence, and a belief in one's ability to overcome obstacles.

Optimistic individuals are more likely to persevere in the face of challenges, maintain focus on their goals, and attract supportive circumstances that contribute to successful manifestation.

Examples of How Emotional Regulation Has Led to Successful Manifestation

Career Advancement: An individual practicing emotional regulation and maintaining a positive mindset may manifest career advancement opportunities by consistently demonstrating enthusiasm, competence, and a proactive attitude at work. By managing stress, staying focused on goals, and cultivating supportive relationships, they attract promotions, recognition, and opportunities for growth and development.

Relationships: Emotional regulation plays a crucial role in attracting and maintaining fulfilling relationships. Someone who radiates love, kindness, and appreciation is more likely to manifest harmonious connections with others. By releasing attachment to past hurts, forgiving, and approaching relationships with openness and authenticity, they attract loving, supportive partners who reflect their positive energy.

Health and Well-being: Effective emotional regulation can positively impact physical health and well-being. Someone who practices gratitude, mindfulness, and self-care may manifest improved health outcomes, vitality, and resilience. By reducing stress, nurturing positive emotions, and adopting healthy lifestyle habits, they attract wellness, vitality, and a sense of wholeness into their lives.

Financial Abundance: Emotional regulation is essential for manifesting financial abundance and prosperity. Individuals who maintain a mindset of abundance, gratitude, and confidence attract wealth and opportunities for financial success. By releasing limiting beliefs about money, cultivating a sense of deservingness, and taking inspired action towards financial goals, they manifest abundance in various forms, including income, investments, and opportunities for wealth creation.

Emotional regulation is a key component of successful mani-festation, influencing our vibrational alignment with desired outcomes, enhancing neural connectivity and manifestation potential, and shaping our experiences in various life domains. By cultivating positive emotions, managing negative emotions, and aligning thoughts and actions with intentions, individuals can harness the power of emotions to manifest their dreams and create a life of fulfillment, abundance, and joy.

IX

Case Studies and Scientific Evidence

25

Neuroscientific Studies

In this chapter, we delve into case studies and scientific evidence that support the intersection between neuroscience and manifestation. We present key studies linking thought processes to real-world changes, discuss research on neuroplasticity, visualization, and the placebo effect, and provide a critical analysis of the evidence supporting the neuroscience of manifestation.

Study 1: Neuroplasticity and Brain Rewiring:

Research: A landmark study conducted by Dr. Michael Merzenich and colleagues at the University of California, San Francisco, demonstrated the brain's remarkable ability to rewire itself in response to experience.

Findings: Through neuroplasticity, the brain can form new neural connections and reorganize existing ones, leading to changes in behavior, perception, and cognition. This study provided compelling evidence for the malleability of the brain and its potential for transformation through intentional practices.

Study 2: Visualization and Motor Skills Enhancement:

Research: Studies in sports psychology have consistently shown the effectiveness of visualization techniques in improving motor skills and performance in athletes.

Findings: Visualization activates similar brain regions as physical practice, leading to enhanced neural connectivity and muscle memory. Athletes who regularly visualize successful performance scenarios demonstrate improved execution and confidence in real-world competitions.

Study 3: Placebo Effect and Healing Responses:

Research: Research on the placebo effect has revealed the profound impact of belief and expectation on physiological responses and healing outcomes.

Findings: Placebo interventions, ranging from sugar pills to sham surgeries, have been shown to elicit real physiological changes in the body, such as pain relief, reduced inflammation, and improved subjective well-being. These findings underscore the influence of mindset and belief systems on health and healing.

Discussion of Research Findings

Neuroplasticity and Manifestation Potential

Analysis: Studies on neuroplasticity highlight the brain's ability to adapt and change in response to focused intention and repetitive mental practices.

Implications: By consciously directing thoughts and engaging in visualization exercises, individuals can rewire their brains to support the manifestation of desired outcomes. This underscores the importance of consistent mental conditioning and deliberate intention-setting in the manifestation process.

Visualization and Reality Manifestation

Analysis: Research demonstrating the effectiveness of visualization in enhancing performance suggests a direct link between mental imagery and real-world outcomes.

Implications: Visualization techniques can be leveraged to align thoughts, beliefs, and actions with desired manifestations. By vividly imagining desired outcomes and embodying the corresponding emotions, individuals can accelerate the manifestation process and increase the likelihood of success.

Placebo Effect and Mind-Body Connection

Analysis: The placebo effect highlights the intricate relationship between mind and body, demonstrating the power of belief and expectation in influencing physiological responses.

Implications: Belief in one's ability to manifest desired outcomes can activate the mind-body connection, leading to tangible changes in health, behavior, and circumstances. By cultivating positive beliefs and maintaining a mindset of abundance, individuals can tap into this innate capacity for self-healing and transformation.

Critical Analysis of the Evidence

Strengths

Empirical Support: Numerous studies provide empirical evidence linking thought processes to real-world changes, validating the principles of manifestation from a neuroscientific perspective.

Practical Applications: The findings offer practical insights into how intentional thought practices, such as visualization and affirmation, can influence neural pathways and shape outcomes in various domains of life.

Limitations

Complexity of Factors: The manifestation process is influenced by multiple factors beyond neural mechanisms, including social, environmental, and situational variables.

Need for Further Research: While existing studies provide valuable insights, more research is needed to elucidate the mechanisms underlying manifestation and explore individual differences in responsiveness to mental practices.

The convergence of neuroscience and manifestation offers a compelling framework for understanding the power of thought in shaping reality. Key studies on neuroplasticity, visualization, and the placebo effect provide robust evidence supporting the connection between mental processes and tangible outcomes. By critically analyzing this evidence, we gain deeper insights into the mechanisms underlying manifestation and its practical implications for personal growth, well-being, and success.

26

Success Stories

In this section, we explore case studies of individuals who have successfully utilized manifestation techniques backed by neuroscience principles. These stories provide detailed accounts of their experiences, the scientific principles involved, and the common factors that contributed to their success.

Case Study 1: Sarah's Career Advancement

Background: Sarah, a marketing professional in her mid-30s, was feeling stagnant in her career and yearned for advancement opportunities. Despite her skills and qualifications, she struggled to break through to the next level.

Manifestation Technique: Sarah decided to apply visualization techniques supported by neuroscience principles to manifest her career goals. She created a detailed mental image of herself excelling in her desired role, visualizing specific tasks, interactions, and achievements associated with success.

Scientific Principles: Sarah's visualization practice tapped into the brain's neuroplasticity, rewiring neural pathways associated with confidence, competence, and goal attainment. By vividly imagining herself in her desired role, she activated brain regions linked to motivation, focus, and skill acquisition.

Experience: Over several weeks of consistent visualization practice, Sarah noticed subtle shifts in her mindset and behavior. She felt more confident in meetings, took on leadership roles in projects, and proactively sought out opportunities for growth.

Outcome: Within a few months, Sarah's efforts paid off as she was offered a promotion to a managerial position. Her visualization practice had helped her align her thoughts, emotions, and actions with her career goals, leading to tangible success.

Case Study 2: David's Financial Abundance

Background: David, a freelance graphic designer, struggled with financial insecurity and debt. Despite his talent and hard work, he found it challenging to attract lucrative projects and stable income streams.

Manifestation Technique: Inspired by research on the placebo effect and the power of belief, David decided to cultivate a mindset of abundance and prosperity. He began practicing gratitude daily, focusing on the financial resources he already had and expressing gratitude for future abundance.

Scientific Principles: David's gratitude practice stimulated the release of neurotransmitters associated with positive emotions, such as dopamine and serotonin. These neurochemicals enhanced his mood, outlook, and receptivity to opportunities for financial growth.

Experience: As David continued his gratitude practice, he noticed a gradual shift in his relationship with money. He felt more optimistic about his financial prospects, took proactive steps to improve his business skills, and networked with potential clients and collaborators.

Outcome: Within a year, David's financial situation dramatically improved. He secured high-paying projects, built a steady client base, and achieved financial stability. His consistent practice of gratitude had transformed his mindset and behavior, leading to tangible results.

Common Factors Contributing to Success

Consistency: Both Sarah and David maintained consistent practices aligned with their manifestation goals, whether it was visualization or gratitude. Regularity and persistence are key factors in rewiring neural pathways and shifting beliefs.

Alignment: They ensured that their thoughts, emotions, and actions were in harmony with their desired outcomes. By cultivating positive emotions and focusing on abundance, they created an energetic resonance conducive to manifestation.

Belief: Sarah and David possessed a deep-seated belief in the effectiveness of manifestation techniques backed by neuroscience. Their unwavering faith in the power of their practices fueled their motivation and resilience in the face of challenges.

Action: While visualization and gratitude played significant roles, both individuals also took tangible actions aligned with their goals. They seized opportunities, expanded their skill sets, and remained open to new possibilities, amplifying the effects of their manifestation practices.

Sarah and David's success stories demonstrate the transformative potential of manifestation techniques grounded in neuroscience principles. By applying these practices with intention, belief, and action, individuals can manifest their desires and create fulfilling lives aligned with their deepest aspirations. Their experiences underscore the profound connection between mind and reality, offering inspiration and guidance for others on their manifestation journeys.

27

Critiques and Challenges

In this section, we address skepticism and challenges in the field of manifestation backed by neuroscience, providing a balanced view that acknowledges both the potential and limitations of current research. We discuss the need for further studies to expand our understanding and encourage critical thinking and an open-minded approach to exploring manifestation.

Addressing Skepticism

Scientific Rigor: Skeptics often question the scientific rigor and validity of studies supporting the neuroscience of manifestation. They may argue that many findings are based on small sample sizes, lack robust experimental designs, or fail to adequately control for confounding variables.

Confirmation Bias: Critics suggest that individuals who believe in manifestation may interpret subjective experiences and anecdotal evidence as validation of their beliefs, leading to confirmation bias. They emphasize the importance of empirical evidence and skepticism in evaluating claims about the effectiveness of manifestation techniques.

Acknowledging Limitations

Complexity of Phenomena: Manifestation is a multifaceted phenomenon influenced by numerous factors, including individual beliefs, environmental influences, and societal structures. Current research often simplifies these complexities, making it challenging to draw definitive conclusions about causality.

Variability in Responses: Not everyone responds to manifestation techniques in the same way, and individual differences in personality, psychology, and neurobiology can influence outcomes. Research must account for this variability and explore factors that moderate the effectiveness of manifestation practices.

Need for Further Studies

Longitudinal Research: Many studies on manifestation are cross-sectional or short-term, providing limited insight into the sustained effects of mental practices over time. Longitudinal research is needed to assess the durability and long-term impact of manifestation techniques on behavior, well-being, and life outcomes.

Mechanistic Understanding: While studies demonstrate correlations between mental practices and neural changes, the underlying mechanisms remain poorly understood. Future research should employ advanced neuroimaging techniques and experimental designs to elucidate the neurobiological processes involved in manifestation.

Encouraging Critical Thinking

Evaluate Evidence: It's essential to critically evaluate the evidence supporting manifestation practices, considering the quality of research, potential biases, and alternative explanations. Adopting a skeptical yet open-minded approach allows for a more nuanced understanding of the phenomena under investigation.

Experimentation and Self-Reflection: Individuals interested in manifestation should engage in personal experimentation and self-reflection to determine what techniques resonate with them and produce meaningful results. Maintaining a spirit of curiosity and self-inquiry fosters ongoing growth and discovery.

While research on manifestation backed by neuroscience offers promising insights into the relationship between mind and reality, it is not without its critiques and challenges. By acknowledging the limitations of current research, advocating for further studies, and encouraging critical thinking, we can foster a more robust and evidence-based understanding of manifestation practices. Ultimately, an open-minded yet discerning approach allows us to explore the potential of manifestation while remaining grounded in scientific inquiry and rational skepticism.

X

Practical Applications and Techniques

28

Daily Practices for Manifestation

In this chapter, we provide practical guidance for integrating neuroscience-based manifestation techniques into daily life. We offer a structured routine for readers to follow, including meditation, visualization, and intention setting, and emphasize the importance of consistency and persistence in achieving results.

Morning Routine

Meditation: Begin your day with a short meditation session to cultivate a calm and focused mind. Sit comfortably, close your eyes, and focus on your breath. Notice any thoughts or sensations that arise without judgment, and gently bring your attention back to your breath. Aim for 5-10 minutes of mindful meditation.

Visualization Exercise

Visualization: After meditation, take a few minutes to visualize your goals and intentions. Imagine yourself achieving your desires in vivid detail, engaging all your senses. Feel the emotions associated with success, and believe in the possibility of your manifestations coming to fruition.

Setting Intentions

Intention Setting: Write down your intentions for the day, focusing on specific outcomes you wish to manifest. Use affirmative language and visualize yourself already experiencing these outcomes. Review your intentions regularly throughout the day to reinforce your commitment.

Midday Check-In

Mindfulness Break: Take a short break in the middle of the day to practice mindfulness. Close your eyes, take a few deep breaths, and tune into your present moment experience. Notice any tension or stress in your body and allow it to release as you breathe deeply.

Evening Reflection

Gratitude Practice: Before bed, reflect on the day and write down three things you are grateful for. Focus on moments of joy, success, and connection. Cultivating gratitude shifts your focus from scarcity to abundance, reinforcing a positive mindset for manifestation.

Structured Routine for Manifestation

Consistent Practice: Commit to practicing manifestation techniques daily, even if only for a few minutes. Consistency is key to rewiring neural pathways and aligning your subconscious mind with your conscious intentions.

Integration: Integrate manifestation practices into your existing daily routine to make them more sustainable. For example, meditate before or after your morning shower, visualize during your commute, and set intentions before starting work or engaging in creative activities.

Adaptability: Be flexible and open to adapting your manifestation routine based on your evolving needs and circumstances. Experiment with different techniques and adjust your practices as you learn what works best for you.

Importance of Consistency and Persistence

Neuroplasticity: Consistent practice of manifestation techniques leverages the brain's neuroplasticity to create lasting changes in thought patterns and behavior. Repetition strengthens neural connections associated with desired outcomes, making manifestation more likely.

Resilience: Persistence in manifestation practices builds resilience in the face of challenges and setbacks. By maintaining a positive mindset and focusing on solutions rather than problems, you become more adept at navigating obstacles and staying aligned with your goals.

Compound Effects: Over time, the cumulative effects of consistent practice compound, leading to exponential growth and progress toward your manifestations. Each small step forward reinforces your belief in the process and increases your momentum toward success.

By integrating neuroscience-based manifestation techniques into your daily routine and prioritizing consistency and per-sistence, you can harness the power of your mind to create positive change in your life. Through meditation, visualiza-tion, intention setting, and gratitude practice, you cultivate a mindset of abundance, resilience, and alignment with your deepest desires. Remember that manifestation is a journey, and by staying committed to your practice, you can manifest the life you truly desire.

29

Exercises and Workbooks

In this section, we provide practical exercises, worksheets, and reflection prompts to support readers in their manifestation journey. These activities are designed to facilitate goal setting, visualization, and tracking progress, encouraging readers to document their experiences and reflect on their growth along the way.

Goal Setting Exercise

Reflective Journaling: Take some time to reflect on your long-term and short-term goals. Write them down in your manifestation journal, being as specific and detailed as possible. Consider what you truly desire in various areas of your life, such as career, relationships, health, and personal development.

SMART Goals Worksheet: Use the SMART criteria (Specific, Measurable, Achievable, Relevant, Time-bound) to refine your goals. Create a worksheet where you outline each goal according to these criteria, breaking them down into actionable steps and setting deadlines for completion.

Visualization Practice

Guided Visualization Meditation: Find a quiet space where you can relax without distractions. Close your eyes and imagine yourself achieving one of your goals. Engage all your senses as you vividly visualize the experience, focusing on the emotions and sensations associated with success.

Vision Board Creation: Create a vision board that represents your goals and aspirations visually. Gather images, quotes, and symbols that resonate with your desires and arrange them on a board or in a digital collage. Display your vision board in a prominent place where you can see it daily.

Progress Tracking Exercise

Daily Manifestation Log: Keep a daily log of your manifestation practices and experiences. Note down any insights, synchronicities, or signs that you observe throughout the day. Reflect on how your thoughts and actions align with your goals and intentions.

Weekly Reflection: Set aside time each week to reflect on your progress and challenges. Use a reflection prompt such as "What went well this week?" and "What can I improve or adjust moving forward?" Write down your reflections in your manifestation journal to track your growth over time.

Affirmation and Gratitude Practice

Morning Affirmations: Start your day with positive affirmations that align with your goals and intentions. Repeat affirmations such as "I am worthy of success" or "I attract abundance into my life" to program your subconscious mind for manifestation.

Gratitude Journaling: End each day by writing down three things you are grateful for. Cultivate a mindset of gratitude by focusing on the blessings and abundance in your life. Notice how expressing gratitude shifts your perspective and enhances your sense of well-being.

These exercises and workbooks provide practical tools for readers to apply neuroscience-based manifestation techniques in their daily lives. By engaging in goal setting, visualization, progress tracking, affirmation, and gratitude practices, readers can deepen their understanding of manifestation principles and accelerate their journey toward realizing their dreams. Remember to stay consistent, be patient with yourself, and celebrate each step forward on your path to manifestation success.

30

Long-term Strategies

In this section, we offer strategies for maintaining a manifestation practice over the long term. We discuss the importance of continuous learning and adaptation, and provide resources for further exploration and support to sustain your manifestation journey.

Consistency and Persistence

Daily Rituals: Establish daily rituals for manifestation that become integrated into your routine. Consistency is key to reinforcing neural pathways and maintaining alignment with your goals.

Accountability: Find an accountability partner or join a manifestation group where you can share your progress, experiences, and challenges. Accountability fosters commitment and motivation to stay on track with your practice.

Continuous Learning and Adaptation

Educational Resources: Stay informed about the latest research, books, and courses on manifestation and neuroscience. Continuously expanding your knowledge base allows you to refine your techniques and deepen your understanding of manifestation principles.

Experimentation: Be open to experimenting with different manifestation techniques and approaches to see what resonates best with you. Adapt your practices based on your evolving needs, preferences, and experiences.

Mindset and Belief

Cultivating Belief: Cultivate a strong belief in the power of manifestation and your ability to create positive change in your life. Trust in the process and believe in the inherent potential within yourself to manifest your desires.

Overcoming Doubt: Address any limiting beliefs or doubts that arise along the way. Practice self-awareness and challenge negative thought patterns by reframing them into positive affirmations and empowering beliefs.

Self-care and Well-being

Holistic Approach: Take a holistic approach to manifestation by prioritizing self-care and well-being. Nurture your physical, emotional, and mental health through practices such as exercise, mindfulness, healthy nutrition, and adequate rest.

Stress Management: Manage stress effectively to maintain

a clear and focused mindset. Incorporate stress-reduction techniques such as meditation, deep breathing exercises, and time spent in nature to promote relaxation and balance.

Resources for Further Exploration and Support

Books: Explore books on manifestation, neuroscience, and personal development for in-depth insights and practical guidance. Some recommended titles include "Breaking the Habit of Being Yourself" by Dr. Joe Dispenza and "The Power of Your Subconscious Mind" by Joseph Murphy.

Online Courses: Enroll in online courses or workshops that delve into manifestation techniques and neuroscience principles. Platforms like Udemy, Coursera, and Mindvalley offer a variety of courses taught by experts in the field.

Community Support: Join online forums, social media groups, or local meetups dedicated to manifestation and personal growth. Surrounding yourself with like-minded individuals provides inspiration, encouragement, and a sense of belonging on your manifestation journey.

Professional Guidance: Consider working with a manifestation coach or therapist who can provide personalized support and guidance tailored to your specific goals and challenges.

Maintaining a manifestation practice over the long term requires dedication, commitment, and a willingness to adapt and grow. By incorporating consistency, continuous learning, mindset cultivation, self-care, and accessing resources for support, you can sustain your manifestation journey and manifest the life of your dreams. Remember that manifestation is a lifelong process of evolution and self-discovery, and each step you take brings you closer to realizing your highest potential.

31

Conclusion

In this concluding section, we summarize the key points discussed in the book, reinforce the connection between neuroscience and manifestation, offer encouragement for practice, and suggest future directions for exploration and research.

Summary of Key Points

Throughout this book, we have explored the fascinating intersection between neuroscience and manifestation, uncovering the powerful connection between the mind and reality. Here are the main concepts we have discussed:

Understanding Neuroscience: We began by introducing basic concepts in neuroscience, exploring how the brain works and its relevance to manifestation practices.

Energy of Thoughts: We delved into the electromagnetic activity of the brain, brainwave patterns, and the measurement of thought energy, highlighting the role of brain activity in shaping reality.

Neuroplasticity and Mindset: We discussed the concept of neuroplasticity and its implications for rewiring the brain to support positive thinking and manifestation. Growth mindset, visualization, and intention setting emerged as powerful tools for neural rewiring.

Emotional Regulation: We explored the impact of emotions on manifestation and discussed techniques for emotional control and resilience, emphasizing the importance of cultivating positive emotional states.

Practical Applications: We provided practical exercises, visualization techniques, and daily rituals for manifestation, encouraging readers to integrate neuroscience-based practices into their lives.

Reinforcement of Connection

The exploration of neuroscience has provided compelling evidence for the connection between thoughts, emotions, and outcomes. By understanding how the brain processes information and forms neural connections, we gain insight into how our thoughts shape our reality.

Encouragement for Practice

Now that you have gained knowledge and insights into the neuroscience of manifestation, it's time to apply what you have learned and observe the impact in your life. Here are some motivational tips to stay committed to your practice:

Consistency is Key: Remember that manifestation is a journey, and progress takes time. Stay consistent with your practices, even on days when motivation is low.

Trust the Process: Trust in the power of your thoughts and intentions to create positive change. Believe in your ability to manifest your desires, and stay focused on your goals.

Celebrate Progress: Celebrate even the smallest victories along the way. Acknowledge your achievements and milestones, and use them as fuel to propel you forward.

Future Directions

As you continue your journey of manifestation, consider these areas for further exploration and research:

Advanced Techniques: Explore advanced manifestation techniques, such as energy healing, subconscious reprogramming, and quantum manifestation, to deepen your practice and expand your understanding.

Interdisciplinary Studies: Explore interdisciplinary approaches that integrate neuroscience with other fields such as psychology, spirituality, and quantum physics to gain new insights into the nature of consciousness and reality.

Personal Growth: Embrace personal growth as an ongoing process, and stay curious and open-minded in your exploration of manifestation. Be willing to evolve and adapt your practices as you gain new insights and experiences.

In conclusion, the journey of manifestation is a profound exploration of the mind's potential to shape reality. By integrating neuroscience-based practices into your life and staying committed to your growth, you have the power to manifest the life of your dreams. Stay curious, stay open, and embrace the infinite possibilities that lie ahead.

Made in the USA
Monee, IL
28 December 2024

75597205R00089